Q

A Dancer's Steps

A Ballet Journal and Workbook

Nancy Bailey Foley
© 2011

Use this book in any way that calls to your creativity. It was designed to help you grow along your journey in dancing. If you write about what you are doing now, it will help you focus on the areas in which you need to improve. And equally important, it will provide you in the future with a snapshot of where you are now. Sometimes as we dance, we hear only the criticism and forget to celebrate how far we've come. You will be able to see your progress and truly appreciate it. Have fun!

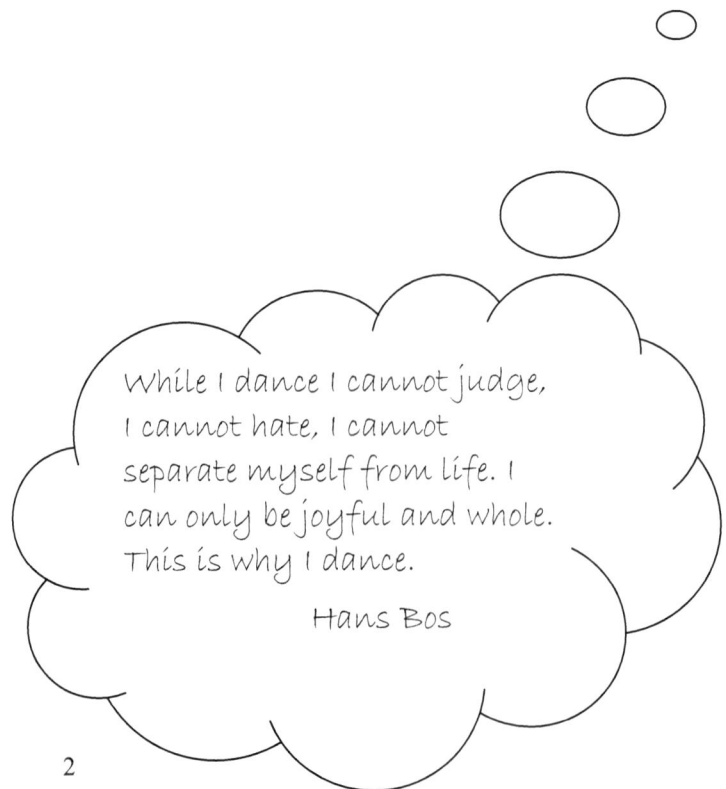

While I dance I cannot judge,
I cannot hate, I cannot
separate myself from life. I
can only be joyful and whole.
This is why I dance.
            Hans Bos

My Ballet Book

Name:

Address:

Phone:

E-mail:

Ballet Class:

Instructor:

Date:

Created by Nants Foley inspired by the talented students of The San Benito Dance Academy in Hollister, California

© Nants Foley 2011

Things I do Well

> Then come the lights shining on you from above. You are a performer. You forget all you learned, the process of technique, the fear, the pain, you even forget who you are. You become one with the music, the lights, indeed one with the dance.
>
> — Shirley MacLaine

Corrections from my Teacher

Technical perfection is insufficient. It is an orphan without the true soul of a dancer.

Sylvie Guillam

Goals

When setting goals for ballet it is important to be SMART about it. Goals which bring our dreams come true are:

SPECIFIC: I want to do the splits by the end of the year. (Not: I want to be more flexible.)

MEASUREABLE: Either you can do the splits or you can't. (How do you measure "more flexible"?)

ACHIEVABLE: It is entirely possible for most people to do the splits.

REALISTIC: (Not: I want to do the splits by tomorrow.)

TIMELY: You need to set a deadline. Dreams without a time limit are merely wishes.

Use SMART goals for achieving whatever you want in life.

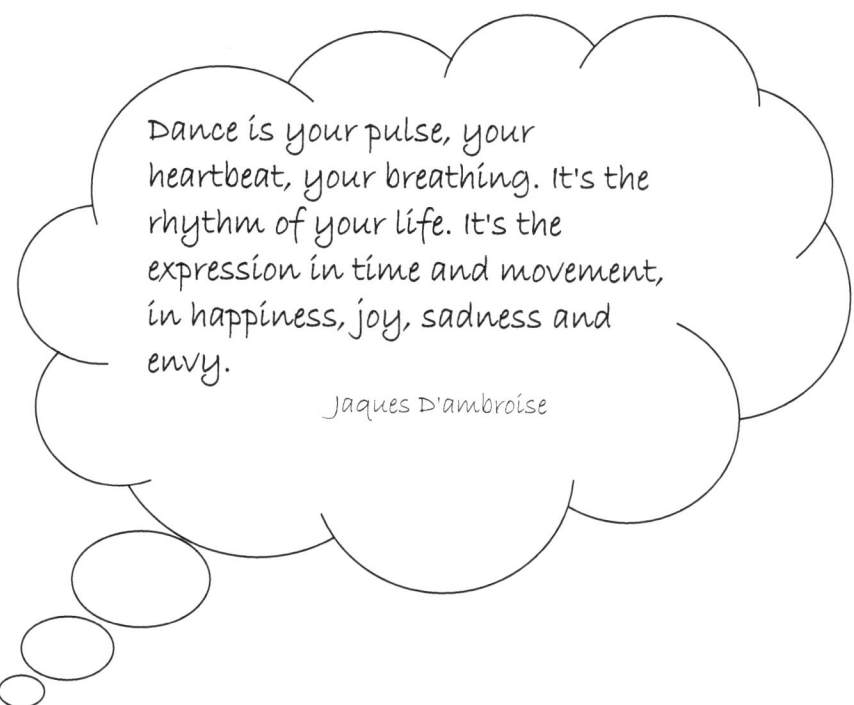

Dance is your pulse, your heartbeat, your breathing. It's the rhythm of your life. It's the expression in time and movement, in happiness, joy, sadness and envy.

Jaques D'ambroise

What I am Working on Now

My Goal	I will: By date:	Work Required:
		Resources needed:
		Challenges to Consider:

What I Like Best About Ballet

Basic Classical Ballet Vocabulary

Adagio — (ah-DAHZ-io) Slow, fluid exercises which develop the dancer's strength and grace.

Allegro – Quick jump combinations

En L'Air — (on lehr) In the air.

Arabesque— (ah-ra-BESK) - The position of the body on one leg with the opposite leg extended behind the body. The arms are held in various positions to create a long, lovely line of the body.

Assemble— (ah-sahm-BLAY) A step in which the working foot slides along the ground before sweeping into the air. Push off the floor with the supporting leg, pointing the toes. Both legs come together in the fifth position in the air to land. Assemble means to assemble.

Attitude— A pose on one leg with the other lifted and bent at approximately a 120-degree angle.

Balance— (ba-iahn-SAY) A swaying step where the weight shifts from one foot to the other.

Chaines— (sheh-NAY) A series of quick traveling turns on demi-pointe in first positions. Literal translation is chains.

Changement- (shahnzh-MAHN) A step beginning in fifth position demi-plié, springing straight up, changing the position of the feet in the air and landing with the opposite foot front in fifth position demi-plie.

Chassé— (shah-SAY) A connecting step where one foot literally chases the other and comes to a fifth position before landing. Literal translation is chased

Coupé — (koo-PAY) A small step often done as a preparation for another step. One foot displaces the other. Literal translation is to cut.

Degage— (day-ga-ZHAY) The working leg brushes the foot against the floor briskly to a slightly raised, pointed position and then closes.

Demi-plié — (duh-mee plee-AY) One of the basic steps of ballet. It entails bending the knees over the toes, keeping the heels on the floor, and increasing turnout at the hips.

Demi-pointe— (duh-mee PWENT) The dancer is to stand high on the ball of the feet.

Développé— (dayv-law-PAY) The working leg is drawn up through a retire position to an open, extended position en l'air. The hips are always kept level and square to the direction that the dancer is facing. Literal translation is to develop.

Downstage - Toward the audience, or in a classroom, the front of the room.

Echappé — (ay-sha-PAY) A movement done from first or fifth to second or fourth position and then closing back to first or fifth.

En Dedans— (aim duh-DAHN) The leg moves in a circular direction, for the right foot counter-clockwise from back to front, and for the left foot clockwise from back to front.

En Dehors— (ahn duh-AWR) The leg moves in a circular direction, for the right foot clockwise from front to back and for the left foot counter clockwise.

Fondu— (fawn-DEW) The standing leg does a demi-plié while the working leg goes to a coupe position and then extends through attitude to a full extension while the standing leg simultaneously straightens. Literally, to melt.

Frappé— (fra-PAY) A dancer forcefully extends the working leg from a flexed coupé position to the front, side or back. This exercise strengthens the toes and instep and develops the dancer's power of elevation. Literal translation is to strike.

Glissade — (glee-SAHD) A linking step executed by gliding the working foot from fifth position demi-plié, pushing off the standing leg, coming to two lengthened legs in the air at once and then landing one leg at a time into fifth position demi-plié. This step is used in petit allegro and grand allegro, and may be used in any direction. Literal translation is to glide.

Jeté— (zhuh-TAY) In petit allegro, this step is executed from a fifth position demi-plie. The dancer does a degage in plie with the working foot, pushes off the standing leg straight up and then lands on the working leg with the standing leg in a coupé position. In a grand allegro, this step is executed by brushing the leg high into the air, pushing off the back leg and performing a "leap." Literal translation is thrown.

Pas de bourrée — (pah duh boo-RAY). This versatile step may be done in various ways and in various directions. It consists of 3 steps, with the first two of on demi-pointe.

Pas de Chat- (pah duh shah) A jump from fifth position demi-plié that brings both legs into a retire position before landing one after the other into a fifth position demi-plié. Literal translation is step of the cat

Passé— (pa-SAY) Movement in which usually begins in fifth position. The working leg is drawn up the standing leg, passes the knee and then closes in the opposite fifth position. Passé resembles retire but differs in that this step changes fifth positions. Literal translation is to pass.

Piqué— (pee-KAY) Step directly onto the demi-pointe of one foot with a push from plie of the other foot in any direction. Literal translation is to pick.

Pirouette— (peer-WET) A complete turn of the body on one foot on the demi-pointe with the other foot usually drawn into a passé position. A pirouette may be done in arabesque or attitude also. A preparation using the demi-plié always proceeds the pirouette. Pirouettes may be done en dehors or en dedans. Literal translation is to whirl.

Port de Bras— (por dih BRAH) The movement and carriage of the arms.

Preparation— The movement with which the dancers gets ready for the dance or exercise to come.

Relevé— (rih-leh-VAY) A raising of the body onto the ball of the foot (demi-pointe) which is done in all positions. Literal translation is raised.

Retire — A position in which the thigh is raised to the second position en l'air so that the toe is in line with and touching the knee of the supporting leg either in front or in back. Retire resembles passé but differs because it usually is a position that comes to the knee and extends to another position rather that closing like the passé. Literal translation is withdrawn.

Révérence — (ray-vay-RAHNSS) Curtsey or bow to the teacher or accompanist.

Rond de Jambe — (rawn duh zhahnb) Circular movement of the working leg. This is done a terre or en l'air, en dehors or en dedans. Literal translation is round of the leg.

Sauté— (son-TAY) Jump, jumping.

Sous-sus— (soo-SEW) A relevé in fifth position that springs to demi-pointe, drawing the feet together with the heels well forward giving the impression of on one foot.

Soutenu en Tournant— A sustained turn in fifth position. Is executed in many different ways.

Spotting- The movement of the head in turning. The dancer chooses a spot on which to focus the eyes. As the turn is made away from the spot, the dancer snaps the head quickly back to the spot as the body completes the turn. This snapping gives the impression that the face is always turned front and helps prevent the dancer from getting dizzy.

Temps Lie— (tawn lyay) From a tendu position, the weight is shifted from the supporting leg to the extended leg, moving first through a plie in the open position.

Tendu — (tawn-DEW) The foot begins in first or fifth, brushes the floor to a pointed foot and then closes back to either first or fifth.

A Terre— (ah tehr) On the ground.

Upstage— Away from the audience, or in the classroom, towards the back.

Tombé— (tawn-BAY) The body falls forward or backward onto the working leg in a demi-plié. Literal translation is falling down.

Turnout —The ability of a dancer to turn his/her feet and legs out from the hip joints.

> Dance til the stars
> come down from the
> rafters
> Dance, Dance, Dance
> til you drop.
> — W. H. Auden

Basic Ballet Theory from the Cecchetti Council of America

Positions of the feet

1st
2nd
3rd
4th
5th
6th
Open positions: 2nd and 4th
Closed positions: 1st, 3rd, and 5th

Positions of the arms

1st
2nd
Half 2nd
5th low
5th in front
5th high

Movement of the feet

When moving from a closed position to an open position, slide to a point and lower the heel. When moving from an open position to a closed position, point and slide lowering the heel.

Movement of the arms

When moving from a low position to a high position, the arms usually pass through 5th in front. When moving from a high position to a low position, the arms usually pass through 2nd and demi 2nd.

Fixed points of the room

The audience is 5. Facing them, beginning with the right, front corner, count the corners counter-clockwise: 1,2,3,4. Count the walls in the same manner: 5,6,7,8.

Positions of the Body

1. À la quatrieme devant (to the 4th front)
2. À la seconde (to the 2nd)
3. À la quatrieme derrière (the 4th back)
4. Croisé devant, (crossed front)
5. Croisé derrière (crossed back)
6. Ecarté (separated, thrown wide apart)
7. Efface devant (partially front)
8. Efface derrière (partially back)

Traditions

Over time, certain traditions and rituals have become part of ballet dance training. For most studios, the standard is a black leotard, pink tights and pink leather shoes for females, black tights and dance belt and white T shirt and white or black shoes for males.

Students must be on time to class. Missing the first warm ups at the barre can lead to pulled muscles.

Hair should be off the face and neck, preferably in a bun. Jewelry is not worn in class.

There is no food in the classroom, though water may be acceptable. Gum chewing is not allowed. Talking to other students is unacceptable. So is sitting on the floor, playing on the barre, or leaning against the walls or mirror.

When not working, students stand at attention and watch fellow students. The teacher may something to another student which you could use, too.

Some teachers allow warm up clothing and skirts, others do not. It is better to ask ahead of time.

If you lose your way in a combination, never walk off the floor. Attempt to finish. If all else fails, get out of the way of other dancers and stand in a dance pose.

Ballet is an art form and a discipline. Correct behavior in class is part of that discipline.

Barre Work

Adagio Combinations

Dance is the hidden language of the soul.

Martha Graham

Jump Checklist

Temps levé

Changement

Èchappé

Glissade

Assemblé

Sissone

Jeté

Emboîté

Pas de chat

OTHER JUMPS I KNOW:

"When you do dance, I wish you a wave o' the sea, that you might ever do nothing but that"

William Shakespeare

Ballets I Have Seen

Master technique and then forget about it and be natural.

                                        Anna Pavlova

Allegro Combinations

Dessous

Movement with one foot stepping or crossing behind the other.

Dessus

Movement with one foot stepping or crossing in front of the other.

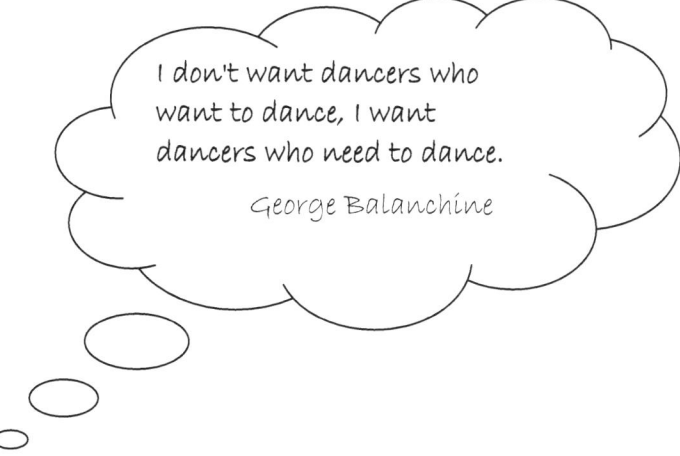

En Dehors

Movement away from the supporting leg.

En Dedans

Movement toward the supporting leg.

He who cannot dance

puts the blame

on the floor.

Hindu proverb

☆

> It is not so much upon the number of exercises, as the care with which they are done, that progress and skill depend.
>
> Auguste Bournonville

Turn Checklist

Détourné

Soutenu

Chaînés

Piqué

Pirouette

Fouetté

OTHER TURNS I KNOW:

> Dance first.
> Think later. It's
> the natural order.
> — Samuel Beckett

Favorite Ballet Music

> I do not try to dance better than anyone else. I only try to dance better than myself.
> — Mihkail Baryshnikov

Favorite Combinations

Musical Vocabulary

Adagio – Slow tempo

Allegro – Lively and fast

Baroque - Time from the middle of the 16th to the middle of the 17th centuries. Characterized by emotional, flowery music in structured form.

Beat - The unit of musical rhythm.

Cadence - A sequence of chords that brings an end to a phrase.

Chord - 3 or 4 notes played simultaneously in harmony

Chromatic scale - Includes all twelve notes of an octave.

Classical - Time from the mid 1700's to mid 1800's. The music was spare and unemotional.

Classicism - Time from the mid 1800's lasting about sixty years. There was focus on order and balance.

Clef - In sheet music, the symbol at the beginning of the staff denoting the pitch of the notes found in the staff.

Coda - Closing section of a movement.

Conductor - Person directing the musicians, indicating the tempo, phrasing, dynamics, and style through gestures and facial expressions.

Dynamics - The loudness or softness of a musical composition and the symbols in sheet music indicating volume.

Energico – Energetically.

Espressivo – Expressively.

Finale - Movement or passage that concludes amusical composition.

Form - The structure of a piece of music.

Forte – Loud.

Grandioso – Grand.

Grave – Slow and serious.

Grazioso – Gracefully.

Instrumentation - Arrangement of music for a number of instruments.

Intermezzo - Short interlude connecting main parts of a composition.

Introduction - The opening section of a piece of music or movement.

Key - System of notes based on and named after the key note.

Key signature - The flats and sharps at the beginning of each staff line indicating the key of the music.

Legato – Smoothly.

Major - One of the two modes of the tonal system, upbeat and positive.

March - A form of music written in two-step time.

Measure - The unit of the staff divided up into two, three, or four beats.

Minor - One of the two modes of the tonal system, usually dark or melancholic.

Movement - A separate section of a larger composition.

Notation - First developed in the 8th century, methods of writing music.

Octave - Eight full tones above the key note where the scale begins.

Orchestra - A large group of instrumentalists.

Overture – The opening of a large piece of music.

Phrase - A single line of music played.

Piano – Softly.

Presto – Very fast.

Renaissance - A period in history from the 14th to 16th centuries which brought the rebirth of music, art, and literature.

Rhythm - The element of music pertaining to time.

Romantic - The 18th and early 19th centuries where the focus shifted from the neoclassical style to an emotional and imaginative style.

Staccato - Short, detached notes.

Staff – The five horizontal parallel lines and the spaces between them on which musical notation is written.

Suite - A loose collection of instrumental compositions.

Tempo – Speed.

Time signature - The numeric symbol in sheet music denoting the number of beats to a measure.

Tone - The intonation, pitch, and modulation of a composition which expresses the meaning and feeling of the music.

Vivace – Lively and spirited.

Waltz - A dance written in triple time with the accent on the first beat of each measure.

Even the ears must dance.

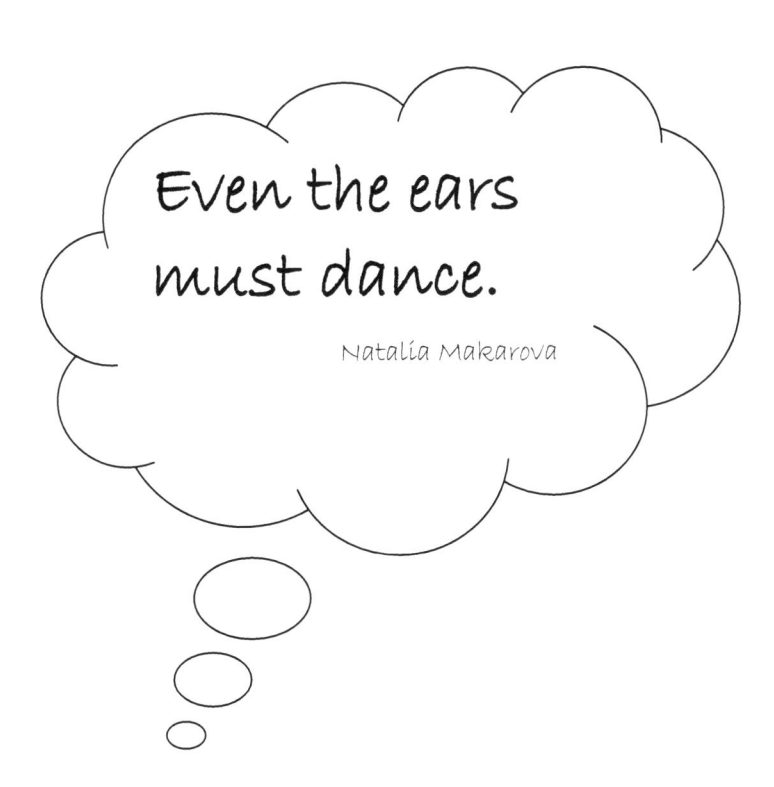

Natalia Makarova

Cross Training

You should consider expanding your physical routine to include a program that addresses muscle development and aerobic fitness. An exercise program of only dancing is not enough.

Researchers have documented that the movements regularly performed by dancers—in class, rehearsal and on stage—last for only brief periods. After testing of ballet dancers' peak oxygen consumption, the researchers found the dancers' cardio-respiratory capacities were similar to other athletes in non-endurance sports.

The soloists had less cardio-respiratory capacity than the corps dancers, presumably because the corps dancers performed for extended periods while the soloists performed for briefer increments with heart rates not sustained for as long a period as the corps de ballet.

The researchers also discovered when the dancers added in other fitness activities, they most often chose Pilates, yoga, or some similar pursuit where the emphasis was more on stretching and not necessarily on aerobics or resistance training.

This lack of a balanced fitness approach often leads to injuries. Add aerobic exercise to your life. A brisk half-hour walk three times a week is a good start.

My Goal	I will:	Work Required:
		Resources needed:
		Challenges to Consider:
	Completion date:	

Good Nutrition is Essential

You must eat - and eat regularly - in order to have the strength and energy a dancer needs. When you are no longer hungry – stop eating. Recognize the signal in you that says you have had enough, and stop. If you eat slowly and chew all your food thoroughly you will give your body time to know when it is no longer hungry.

Choose foods that digest more slowly so they will give you energy over a longer period. Dark, coarser foods such as brown rice, whole grain breads, and yellow vegetables are only a few of the excellent choices you can make. Refined carbohydratess such as white bread, white rice and white sugar are rapidly digested by your body. They will leave you feeling hungry way too quickly. You eat more frequently, adding unnecessary calories to your system but leaving you with less energy. The more processed a food is, the less likely it is to fuel you properly.

Go light on meat, especially red beef. These foods have the protein you need to make new tissue, but they are also extremely high in animal fat which is loaded with calories and the "bad" kind of fat (saturated and trans-fats) which promote plaque build-up in your arteries. A serving size for a meal is about the size of a deck of playing cards. You do need adequate protein to build proper muscle and bone. The best sources are fish, chicken without the skin, and nuts, all of which contain the protein you need.

Stay away from high-fat dairy products. Skim milk and lowfat yogurt give you what you need nutritionally. Also avoid the salt shaker!

Drink 8 glasses of water per day and eat 5 to 7 fresh vegetables and fruits. You'll feel great and look fabulous.

	I will:	Work Required:
My Goal		Resources needed:
		Challenges to Consider:
	By date:	

> We should consider every day lost in which we don't dance.
>
> Nietzsche

Random Thoughts

About My Health

Dancers are the athletes of God.

Albert Einstein

A Perfect Ballet Bun

Spray loose hair with hairspray.

Brush hair into a high ponytail at the crown of the head. Hold ponytail in place with one hand while smoothing out any bumps in the hair leading to the ponytail.

Fasten the ponytail tightly in place with a thick hair elastic band. Shake your head a few times to be sure the ponytail will stay in place.

Twirl ponytail in one direction to form a tight coil. Wrap the coil around the base of the ponytail to begin forming the bun.

As you wrap, secure the coil to the base of the ponytail by sticking V-shaped hair pins through the hair and the hair elastic band, pinning along the outer-most edge of the coil.

Wrap a hairnet around the bun until the hairnet is tight. Fasten with hair pins.

Spray the styled hair with another mist of hairspray. Use hair pins to tuck in stray pieces of hair if necessary.

If your bun comes loose in class, ask to be excused briefly. Go outside the classroom and re-do. This is not a good thing. Your hair should remain as secure during a class as it will be during a performance.

Learning to walk set you free. Learning to dance gives you the greatest freedom of all: to express with your whole self the person you are.

- Melissa Hayden

Foot Care

Soak your feet in a warm, soapy bath to clean the skin and relax the muscles and joints after being on pointe or taking a class. Use Epsom salts to soak your feet if your feet or toes are swollen. Cleaning the feet or using a ballet foot spray soon after dancing helps keep down the risk of developing foot and toe fungus.

Apply thick moisturizing foot balm on your heels and areas where corns, blisters and calluses could develop. Do this every day.

Keep your toe nails trimmed properly. Pointe dancers should not allow their toe nails to be long, but rather trimmed neatly straight across. Do not cut very short or cut into the sides as this could cause ingrown toe nails or other foot problems due to the extreme pressure put on the toes while dancing on pointe.

Wear appropriate padding in your pointe shoes every time you put them on for class, rehearsal or performances. The toe or box area should be padded with either toe pads or lambs' wool.

In life as in dance:
Grace glides on
blistered feet.

— Alice Abrams

Practice Log

Dancing should look easy; like an optical illusion. It should seem effortless. When you do a difficult variation, the audience is aware that it is demanding and that you have the power and strength to do it. But in the end, when you take your bow, you should look as if you were saying, 'Oh, it was nothing. I could do it again.'

-Bruce Marks

What I Think About

Things to Do

My Ballet Friends

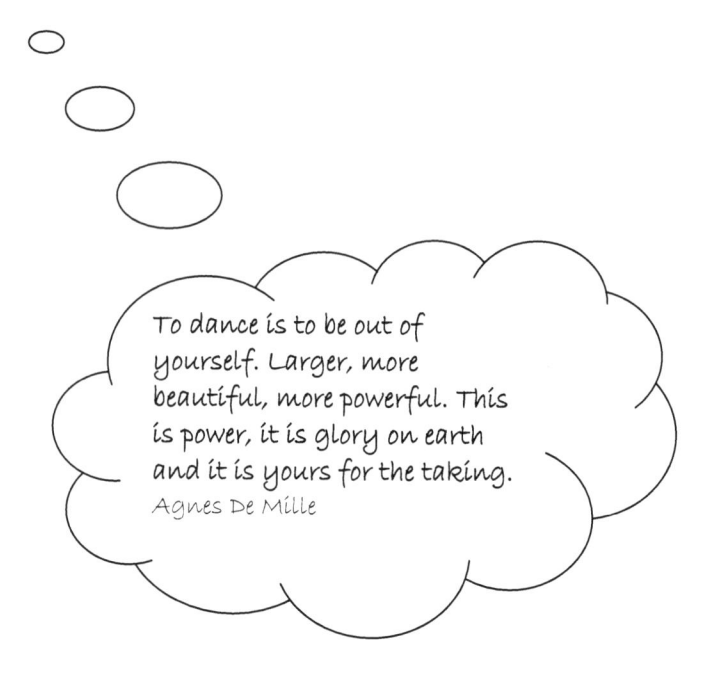

> To dance is to be out of yourself. Larger, more beautiful, more powerful. This is power, it is glory on earth and it is yours for the taking.
> Agnes De Mille

Made in the USA
Charleston, SC
01 September 2011